Eternal Bridges

May God bless you and
reach out to you in these prayers
that He has blessed me with.

John Hartman

ACROSS THE BRIDGE

Lord, across the dark, cold waters,
you have prepared a bridge for me.
Make my steps sure.
Keep my feet dry.
Smooth the way ahead.

Eternal Bridges

PRAYERS TO HELP CANCER
PATIENTS CONNECT WITH GOD

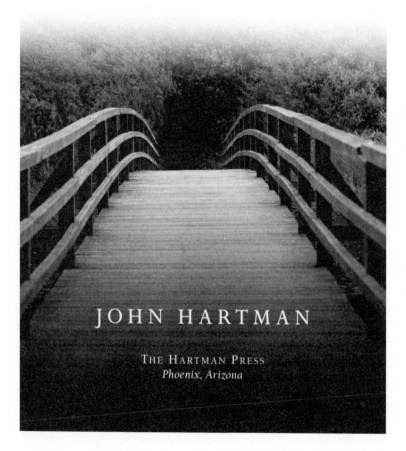

JOHN HARTMAN

THE HARTMAN PRESS
Phoenix, Arizona

For further information contact:

John Hartman

P.O. Box 15653

Phoenix, AZ 85060

e-mail: eternalbridgesprayers@aol.com

www. eternalbridgesprayers.com

Copyright c 2011 by John Hartman

Design: Cindy Kiple

First Edition: August 2011

Library of Congress Control Number: 2011912550

ISBN : 978-09838216-0-1

Printed in the United States of America

1 2 3 4 5 6 7 8 9 10

To Cindy
my hummingbird

Contents

Foreword

As I write these words, my dear friend John Hartman lies in a cancer treatment center in Portland, Oregon, having just received his latest round of chemo. Not knowing what the immediate future holds, he remains firm in his conviction as to who holds that future. John actually called me moments ago to give me a word of encouragement. How typical of the man whom so many have come to love and admire in recent years.

That is what makes the pages of his book unique. You hold in your hands a journal of John's conversations with the Lord as he is walking through his battle with still another cancer diagnosis. It is about John, yet as you read, you discover that this book is not about John at all. The battle is far from private. Because John is writing with the transparency of a humble heart and with a willingness to bare his own soul in Job-like honesty, the reader can find hope when personal fears and pains are laid at the Savior's feet.

Years ago C. H. Spurgeon advised young pastoral students "always to preach to the suffering, and you will never be without a congregation." John in these poignant pages of his journal now speaks to those who are hurting. For that reason alone I trust that its readership will be vast. If you are the one who hurts, I pray that the "God of all comfort" will use these pages to comfort your soul.

John Politan
Scottsdale, Arizona

Introduction

As I BEGAN TO READ the short passages in this book, I was struck by their similarity to the Psalms. Just as David alternated between praising God for the miracles in his life, to crying out to God for help in distress, John Hartman describes both his joys and struggles as he deals with recurrent cancer and its treatment. Adding to the impact is the reality that he is not merely recalling these experiences, he is describing them as they happen—and they are happening not over weeks, or months, but over decades.

There is no question that John's talking with God, as part of having an ongoing relationship with God, is how he made it through each day. Prayer was the key to his survival—and more than just enabling him to survive, it was how he was able to find joy and peace during the grueling process of chemotherapy and its many side effects. John's experience is not an isolated instance, but can be achieved by anyone. This book is a blueprint for that. Whether it is cancer or any other debilitating illness, research shows that when people turn to prayer, their prayers can bring comfort, meaning, and hope. As the situation worsens and stress increases, it seems that faith in God vs. faith in self separates those who are overwhelmed from those who are not. Hundreds of scientific studies demonstrate a connection between religious faith and well-being, happiness, meaning, purpose, as well as having an optimistic attitude in times of crisis. The "peace that passes understanding" can be a reality.

It is seldom an easy ride, however, as John expresses so articulately here. Even for a person with the strongest faith, there are ups and downs. Faith waxes and wanes, as do hope and endurance. Many times the person must cry out to God for more faith, throwing his or her life on God's mercy when all seems bleak. Circumstances often change in response to prayer, as long as the sufferer does not give up but continues to believe that God is the only rock on which to build a future and a hope. Persisting in such situations makes faith strong and develops perseverance.

In *Eternal Bridges*, John's experience adds a real face to the volumes of research that show what faith can do—and is doing all the time. I encourage you to travel on this journey with John as he holds onto his faith and onto God.

Harold G. Koenig, M.D.
Professor of Psychiatry and Behavioral Sciences
Associate Professor of Medicine
Director, Center for Spirituality, Theology and Health
Duke University Medical Center
Durham, North Carolina

Cancer Is Not a Death Sentence

I N THE 1970s, when I first received a cancer diagnosis, the word was simultaneous with a death sentence. Today, almost forty years later, I am well aware that God has had his hand on me year after year. Cancer for me is a Life Sentence. The journey continues.

The year was 1975. I was a senior in college when I noticed a lump in my neck. A biopsy confirmed that it was malignant. Three long weeks later, I learned it was Hodgkin's disease, Stage 1.

The prognosis was good. The disease was confined to my neck. I was able to graduate from college with a degree in Biology Education despite the radiation treatments. I looked forward to marriage, a home, and a career teaching biology and horticulture.

Three years later, some lumps appeared in my groin area. Another biopsy. Malignant! Numerous tests later, including bone marrow extraction, the cytology report indicated Hodgkin's disease again. This time, Stage 3. It had spread above and below my umbilical region. The doctor predicted I had about three months to live. I wasn't willing to accept that verdict and sought a second opinion. A change of doctors gave me hope and a treatment plan.

Six months of MOPP chemotherapy followed. My weight dropped from 205 pounds to 137. The toxicity destroyed most of the major vessels in my hands and arms with complications that would bother me for years. Grueling as it was, it got the job done. The three-month prognosis stretched out to almost thirty years, although they were not easy. The radiation and chemotherapy treatments triggered heart problems and clotting strokes. I stopped teaching, moved around a bit, my marriage ended. I then began a new career as a professional swim coach.

In the spring of 2007, I was rear-ended while stopped at a traffic light. I was taken to the local hospital emergency room where the doctors did blood work that showed an abnormal reading of calcium, commonly the result of malignancy. After that, various doctors poked, prodded, cut, and scanned me, searching for the source of the hypercalcemia. It was close to the end of 2007 before a team of Mayo Clinic specialists reached a diagnosis: Diffuse Large B cell Lymphoma, Stage 4.

I was in for a rough ride. The cancer had spread to ninety percent of my bone marrow, my liver, and throughout the lymphatic system. R-CHOP chemotherapy began right after the first of the year. Rushed to emergency during a severe nadir, I could hear the doctors working frantically to save my life. I could hear my sister Joyce encouraging me to hang on. I heard the Lord saying, "You can come with me and be at peace." I asked him to allow me to live so I could use the gifts he had given me. I struggled during the ongoing therapy, and then slowly I began to heal. My last treatment was April 29, 2008.

It left my hands and feet numb. I was always cold and the peripheral neuropathy was painful. That spring I moved to Phoenix, Arizona, where the warm weather satisfies my body's craving for heat.

Now I was penniless, but the Lord provided for my needs in unexpected ways. Once, when I needed airline tickets to see my oncologist, an unknown benefactor provided them. Her name was Cindy Williams. I offered to treat her to dinner as a way to say thank-you; that meal was the beginning of a special relationship. She is now Cindy Hartman.

Cindy is the most wonderful Christian. Her life inspires me. With Cindy by my side, my faith, prayers, and strength increased.

In May 2009, I penned the first prayer in this book. My story now continues in prayer form.

These prayers reflect my cancer journey. The ups and downs. The pain. The despair. The hopes. The joys. The encouragements. Yes, I also have friends who encourage me. I read the Scriptures daily and they give me joy, peace, hope. I present them here in *Eternal Bridges* from my heart to yours. May the Lord encourage all who read them as he has encouraged me. I have so much to thank him for.

John Hartman
Phoenix, Arizona

The Prayers

RECOVERING

Recovering from chemotherapy.
I need to do more than wait around to heal.
May the Lord give me direction.

I float in a living purgatory

between the pit and the light.

My faith looks upward to you, Lord.

Lord, speak to me.

Tell me your direction for me.

Father, I will go there.

Relieve me from recovery's pain,

the chemo side effects that linger on.

Pain of the flesh.

Pain of the spirit.

REAWAKENING THANKS

Much stronger.
I remember when I could walk only a block.
I remember the wheelchair.
Thank you, Lord.

God of love, you cradle me in your arms.

You provide me with daily bread.

Your shelter protects me

from the turmoil all around me.

Lord, may I always be worthy

of the mercies you give to me.

I am your humble servant

unworthy of holy adorations.

I thank you for your unconditional love,

for giving me another chance.

May 24, 2009

GRACE

Lots of time on my hands.
I pray for a closer walk with Christ.

Dear Father, thank you for
revealing your glorious ways to me.

Without you and your saving grace,
I am a sinner.

Without your edifying Word,
I am bereft.

Without your illuminating glory,
I am blind.

Come, awaken my lethargic heart.
Teach me your righteous ways
that I may walk in your perfect light.
Surround me with your kindness,
discipline me when I fail.
You are my Father.
You alone are holy.

MY NAVIGATOR

The Lord promises to lead me.

Lord, your hand is on the rudder of my life.
I trust you to steer me.
I will not question you.

You are my Guide.
I will not turn away from you.
I want you always close by my side.

EVER CLOSER TO GOD

As I read the Bible and pray daily,
my relationship with the Lord is growing.
This is a good day, so full of grace.

Almighty God, you rule over all.

Your hand is righteous and kind.

Your mysteries befuddle all

who do not know your Word,

who do not have a relationship with you.

As you draw me close to you

and your precious Word,

the mystery clears.

Father, draw me closer.

LOOKING FOR THE LIGHT

Going to Bible study on Sundays.
I realize my imperfections.
I struggle with them
and the agony of cancer's side effects,
every day.

Father, as I bow my head in prayer,

may your salvation shine

on my weary soul,

a soul blinded by disease

and my impatience.

Father, you are the shining beacon

of kindness and safety

in this world of sin.

May I partake of your merciful radiance.

Deliver me from the darkness that lurks

within me and around me.

My love for you weathers

the test of time,

the agony of cancer.

June 14, 2009

WELL ENOUGH TO
BE DISTRACTED

Feeling stronger, but my mind
is wandering toward unhealthy thoughts.
I must be getting well!

Protect me, O Lord, from the evil one.

He's waiting to find a chink in my armor.

Protect my shield of faith from his devious schemes.

Cover it with your mighty hand,

so there's no opening for his wickedness.

FEELING GOD IN MY LIFE

I am beginning to exercise;
it helps me separate
my spiritual life
from my physical life.
I know there is more!

Lord, though my struggles are many,

my faith in you burns strong.

I sense your guiding hand

and kindness toward me

as I wander blindly

through a world of clay feet.

You show me the way

when I am lost.

You never forsake me

when I need you.

I thank you.

FOURTEEN MONTHS CLEAN

The Lord is giving me a normal life.
Fourteen months in remission.
The oncologist tells me the
magic number is twenty-four.

Lord, for you I wait patiently.

Your nourishing Word is the daily bread

that keeps my hungering soul nourished.

I am your beloved,

you feed me,

provide me shelter,

guide my hand.

Your love illuminates my journey.

Lord, I am waiting for you.

July 11, 2009

TRUSTING GOD

Feeling stronger every day.
God is so good.

O Lord, your light, like a beacon,
shines bright from the highest mountain.
It guides my ship.

Its beaming glow shows me the way,
it keeps me from devastating rocks.
Your continuous light pilots my ship
to the safety of your calm harbor.
With faith, I point my bow in your direction.
Even though the storms at sea toss my ship,
I navigate toward your light.
Father, hold my hand on the steerage
as I follow your illuminating beacon.

SORE FEET

Chemotherapy has side effects.
Neuropathy in my hands and feet.
Painful! It's like walking on pointed rocks.

Father in heaven, light of my life,

you give hope to the despondent,

light to those surrounded by darkness,

drink to those who are thirsty.

Though I walk on pointed rocks,

you smooth my path.

When my coffers are empty,

you shower me with wealth.

I will obey you. I will honor you.

I will follow where you lead.

TRANSITIONING

As I read the Bible daily,
I sense God's presence.
It gives me much-needed peace.

Lord, why do you cradle me so close?

Why do you love me so much?

You point north and I go south,

you redirect me and start me north again.

How can you find my wandering ways worthy

of your faithfulness?

Father, teach me to listen to your Word.

Calm my restless soul.

May I always respect your directives.

Give me the strength to serve you

when and where you choose.

JUST A STONE

When I heard my diagnosis last year,
it was like a death sentence.
The Lord intervened.
He has a plan for my life.
Sometimes I'm impatient
as I wait to discover what it is.

O God, Architect of our universe,

Creator of everything, known and unknown.

Right now, I feel like a stone.

Do with me what you will.

Cast me into the sea.

I am yours to throw.

Make me the foundation for a new home.
I am yours to build on.

Place me into the curb of a road.
I am yours to help guide those
in danger of going astray.

Lay me alone on the ocean floor.
Do whatever you will.

I am here because of you.
I am yours.
Place me where you will.

DIVINE MEDICINE

A friend of mine, a Catholic priest,
warns me I will undergo a prolonged affliction.
He advises me to use the time wisely.

Blessed Father, you warm me with your healing light.
Your Word eases the affliction
that threatens to smother my spirit.
Your Word diffuses pain with a peaceful calm.

Lord, open my ears,
my eyes,
my heart.

Your Word is the medicine that treats my malady.
Your tenderness caresses my anxious heart.
I want to please you,
when I stand,
strong and healthy,
before your mercy seat.

July 23, 2009

LIVING IN THE MOMENT

God stopped my life for a while.
The chemo side effects
and multiple surgeries
continue to disable me.
I need to smell the roses.

Lord, every day the light of the sun opens my eyes.

Let me always awaken to its invitation

to celebrate new mercies.

Each day you give me

enables me to enjoy the wonderful peace

that you grant to me.

You are my life; each moment is a lifetime.

May I never take for granted the blessings

you set before me.

SACRED SUMMIT

An appointment with the oncologist
is coming up on August 3.
Cancer free?
More chemotherapy?
It's like going before a firing squad.
They may shoot me with some bad news.
I pray. I pray hard.

Holy Father, high and mighty,

every day humanity climbs and scampers

over each other to find their earthly summit.

Their true summit, however, lies within their being.

Lord, you are the Summit they seek.

You are the Summit I seek.

Show me the path designed for me,

it will lead to true joy and blessing.

Forgive my anxious moments.

I seek your heights of love.

Mold me, Father, to be more like your Son.

PEACE AND PATIENCE

I'm waiting for my medical appointment.
It's hard not to be a clock-watcher.
I need patience. I need peace.

O Lord, on my knees
I pray for just a small grain of your patience.
You alone can satisfy my trembling spirit.
Ease my distress.
You know my thoughts.

Lord, quiet my mind with your Word.
Infuse your peace into my waiting heart.
In the stillness, Lord,
May I be at peace.

LIKE A TODDLER

Feeling calm.
At peace with the Lord.
A toddler in his arms.
Soothing.
I see the oncologist next week.
I will be at peace with the outcome.

Omniscient Father,

who knows all,

make me worthy.

I was blind.

You gave me sight,

yet I still close my eyes

and I wander lost.

You show me the path,

yet I turn the other way.

Father, your patience is humbling.

Forgive me when I close my eyes.

Correct me when I turn the wrong way.

I am like a toddler.

Teach me.

July 31, 2009

GOD'S PURPOSE

Its been months since chemo and surgery.
Still recovering.
Still very weak.
God has his divine purpose.

Lord, many doors you open for me.

Many remedies you provide.

You give me direction

as I wander in the wilderness.

Your love is matchless.

You are always right beside me.

May I follow your footsteps.

Allow me to serve your Kingdom.

May others see your majestic working in my life.

It belongs to you.

Lord, may I walk worthy.

35

SOOTHING ANGELS

Many people provide for my well-being:
my friend Cindy
my sister Joyce
her husband Lee, and their children
Kevin and Debbie, who extended hospitality
Mark and Maureen, who introduced me to Arizona
Dr. Keith Lanier and his medical staff
many more, too numerous to list.

Father, you know all that happens.

You allow the tide to come and go,

the animals to live and die,

the plants to grow and blossom.

You send me angels.

When I thirst, they give me water to drink.

When sad, they offer me hope and love.

When my spirit is broken, pain tearing at my flesh,

they soothe my agony.

God in heaven, bless, protect, and hold close
to your heart these precious angels
who live to protect, love, and care for others.
They give when they have nothing to give.
They hold me tight when they have
no strength and their arms are weak.

Why send these angels to comfort me?
It must be your loving plan.
It's a perfect plan.
May I never forget these precious angels
who lift me up in my great need.
I thank you for them, Father . . . on my knees.

QUIET MY NEEDS

August 3 oncology report unremarkable.
Labs good.
Yet the pain persists.

O Giver of all that is good,

I ask for many things.

Yet who am I to ask?

You bless me with your presence.

You keep me from despair when sick.

Help me, Lord, to overlook my pain,

to be content with your compassionate love.

August 7, 2009

THE PAUSE THAT REFRESHES

God's way is perfect.
Increasingly, I realize that.
During this past year of recovery,
while on the shelf,
I've become more conscious of his presence.
I'm now on the mend.
A better future lies ahead
with Cindy, who is now my fiancée.

God of many blessings,

Divine Creator of all we know.

Affliction interrupted my life.

It stopped me cold with pain and weakness.

Put me on the shelf.

During this time of waiting,

you came to me,

drew me close to you.

May I be worthy of your goodness

as I continue to recover.

Your presence strengthens my soul,

it lessens my pain.

THE LORD'S WEALTH

Feeling almost normal now.
My life is rich.
My friends wonder why I smile so much.

Lord, blessed is the wondrous way
in which you are weaving
the mosaic of my life.
I thank you
for the delicate way you hold me.
Your design for me is perfect.

Many pitied me as my cancer spread.
They shake their heads even as I recover.
They know I am financially impoverished.

They cannot fathom that reading
your Word makes my soul healthy and rich.
The times that I lie alone, barely able to move,
are your blessings to me.

You are sewing golden threads into my weary heart.
Your divine mosaic is perfect.

GOD'S APPROVAL

It's not about me.
It's about him.

Ruler of all the earth,
you weave the day into night and back again.
You have the power to take all, to give all.
I submit to your powerful Word
that gives me strength.

Though I am but one, and can do little,
what I have, I bring to you.
I live for you.
For your approval, by your grace,
I so want to reflect your love.

August 19, 2009

STILL THE POINTED ROCKS

The nagging neuropathic pain
in my feet bugs me.
I need to have further surgery
to attach my abdominal muscles
so I can be more mobile.
Core stability is important
for even minor activity.

O Lord, take away the discomfort.

It awakens with me in the morning,

follows my every step throughout the day.

Your love is the tonic I need.

Come to me.

Comfort me.

On bended knee, I pray for grace.

Take away this distracting pain.

Have mercy on me, Lord.

GOD'S MOUNTAIN

I'm in a valley today, looking up.
It's a long way to the top.

You are the God of all comfort,
look down on your servant today.
As I cope with my infirmities,
your Word soothes my spirit.

You are my pinnacle of peace.
Lead me up the mountain,
away from the valley.

GOD IN MY DAY

I spend time daily with the Lord.
I am so blessed by the Bible Cindy gave me.
It is my constant companion.

Thank you, Lord, for the blessings
   that each new day brings.
With the dawn, your grace
   sprouts new beginnings.
My time with you is so blessed.
You are always there for me.
You speak gently to me.
You comfort me.
Unlike the emptiness of human words,
your Holy Spirit teaches me
rich lessons from your Word.

A CLUTTERED MIND

Now that I'm feeling better,
people try to coax me to be part of their busy lives.
I have been secluded for a long time.
The pressure confuses me.

Humbly, I kneel before you, O Lord,

with a cluttered mind.

It is cluttered with the pressures of a worldly culture.

May your beacon light shine brightly

through the daily rubble I face.

I will follow to your place of rest.

There, my earthly concerns will disappear.

GOD'S DAILY ASSIGNMENTS

I'm living on borrowed time.
I pledge my time to the Kingdom.
Easier said than done.

Father, thank you for influencing my life.

You've given me many opportunities.

Each one is a blessing to me.

Let me not overlook even the smallest assignment.

Give me discernment to recognize the pain of another

so my efforts are a joy to you.

A DAILY CROSS

My life is changing.
Living for God is a learning curve.
Some days it's easy;
other days, it is tough.

Lord Jesus, you tenderly say to me,

"Pick up your cross and follow me."

It's heavy and awkward.

Give me strength to bear its weight.

Hold me steady so I don't stumble.

The journey is long,

the trail is narrow.

THE BUS DRIVER

God controls my life.
He is my Rock,
the foundation of my faith.

Dear God, Father on high,

today I am singing your praises.

My feet burn with pain,

my mind is muddled.

Yet, with faith, my soul burns brightly.

You drive the bus.

I am a passenger.

Occasionally, I switch seats,

but I never touch the wheel.

Drive me where you will.

September 2, 2009

TEMPTATION

Life is moving fast.
Cindy will soon be my wife.
It's easy to be distracted.

You are my Savior.

Shield my eyes,

plug my ears,

quiet my racing mind.

May I listen to your speaking voice.

Dwell on your purity.

Be an example of the believer.

FORGIVENESS

I tend to hold grudges against people who wrong me.
I'm learning to forgive. When I do,
I'm relaxed and peaceful.

Lord Jesus, you not only forgive,

you also forget.

Help me to do the same.

When people wrong me,

remind me to imitate the way you lived.

To forgive.

To forget.

And to love.

ONE LAYER AT A TIME

*Faith is like
peeling an onion,
one layer at a time.*

Your Word is always uplifting.
I cherish the time spent with you
as your Word washes the grime from
my imperfect soul.

You reveal yourself to me
one layer at a time.
In your omniscience, you know
what my soul needs.

Thank you for your unconditional patience
and your tender touch.

FLAWS

Feeling so much better physically.
I want to rule the world.

Lord, look down upon your stumbling servant.

I'm becoming critical.
And greedy.
I'm feeling lofty.
And proud.

Nudge me.
Humble me.
Restrain me.

Show me how to live.

THE LIFEBOAT

*I cannot function
without the Lord's help.*

Lord, without your guiding light,
I am adrift at sea.
I flounder without a boat,
no land in sight.
Tossed to and fro by the pounding waves,
I sink.

Your glorious Word is a lifeboat
that keeps me safe on an endless ocean of sin.
Your forgiving heart is the dry land
on which I bask in your warmth.

PEACE

*All I am and have
comes from God.*

Lord, your beauty is matchless.
Your mercy is perfect.
Brighten my day.
Surround me with peace.
Amen.

CINDY, MY WIFE

September 30, 2009
Our wedding day.
God's plan for us.
May we be worthy.

Father, to you I give thanks.

You've given me Cindy.
A partner for life.
Show us where to walk.

Your power strengthens me.
Your blessings surround me.
Why do you love me so much?

October 6, 2009

CRADLING ARMS

My sister gave me a picture
taken when I was about three years old.
My father was holding me in his arms.
I loved my father.
In his arms, I knew I was safe.

Heavenly Father, there is comfort in your Holy Word.

You cradle me in your arms

when my spiritual fire burns low.

Father, blow on the embers that still burn.

Rekindle the flame again.

May it burn brightly within me.

For all to see.

John in his father's arms.
Summer 1956.

ALMOST A YEAR!

It's been almost a year since chemotherapy.
I thank the Lord.
I ask for continued mercy and endurance.

God from above,

Ruler of heaven and earth,

I give thanks for these days of remission.

Through all those months riddled with pain,

you have comforted me.

I will continue to trust your healing touch.

Show me your will.

I want to serve you.

I want to honor you.

LIFTED UP

I'm finally feeling out of the valley.
Newly married.
Setting up a household.
Resting in his goodness.

Father, you are the source of everything.

You know the minds of all

who walk and who have walked the earth.

You are beyond comparison.

You have lifted me up with your holy hands.

Lord, still my mind as I savor your Word.

Focus my eyes on your guiding light.

Direct my steps to the right assignment for me.

ON TARGET

Choices determine our lives.
Direction is a choice.

O gracious, heavenly Father,
help me on my journey.
Though my legs are heavy,
and my steps are slow,
I walk toward your light.
Lighten my stride when the time is right.

I will look straight ahead,
not to the right, nor to the left.
I will move closer to you,
inch by inch.

LIKE A HUMMINGBIRD

In the daily tumult of life,
I sometimes dart like a hummingbird.

Creator of the universe,
you soar through the heavens
like a majestic eagle
seeing all that is below.

I'm like the flittering movements
of the hummingbird
rapidly going from flower to flower,
never staying in one spot.
Living to find another blossom,
always moving randomly.
Father, slow down my thinking
to concentrate more on you.

THE TIDE

The ebb and flow of pain
does not subside.
It demands my attention.

Lord, your love fills my life
as the sea fills the ocean floors.

My spirit is like the tide.
It flows into you,
then retreats.

Lord, still the waters,
calm my heart.

You are my God.
You are my Savior.
You are my Guide.

Perfect in every way.
Escort me to your shores.

PARADOX

It's important to try.

I may strive for perfection,
but I cannot achieve it.
I am not divine.

You know my struggles.
You know I am trying
to please you.

MAY I BE WORTHY

Over and over,
the Lord blesses me.

Ruler of all that is,
How impeccable is the love you provide.
How glorious is your perfect timing.

Your grace is like
a perfect white cloud
on a sunny day,
shading me
from the scorching heat
of the sun.

O Lord, may I be worthy.
May my squinting eyes
see your path.
Give me strength
and grace
to serve you.

November 26, 2009

November 26, 2009

THANKSGIVING

So much to be thankful for.

Lord, you are my salvation.
You know my innermost thoughts.
Your plan is perfect.

When lonely, your presence comforts me.
When ill, you tenderly soothe me.

Your love is like a warm fire
on a cold winter day.
You accept me as I am.
You are my Heavenly Father.

UNCERTAINTY

PET scan coming up in a few weeks.
My mind wanders . . . "what if?"
Most likely I'm not out of the woods yet.
My faith keeps me calm.

Savior and Friend,
your Word bathes
my parched mind
with clean water,
purifying my soul.

Your Word gives
hope,
courage
in my uncertainties.

Your Word promises
peace,
perseverance
to endure the bitter pain.

QUESTIONING

Still thinking about the PET scan.
Wondering if my battle
with lymphoma is over.

Lord, your ways are right.

You know what is best.

Still, the questions come.

Feeling as if a giant wave might crush me,

push me down to the ocean floor.

You've given me the breath of life.

Now encourage me with your favor.

Help me absorb your Holy Word.

It gives me peace.

It reassures me that you keep your promises.

RAPIDS IN THE SPRING

Patience is not my forte. I want to know
God's plan for me.
I want to know right away.
Please.

Savior, Redeemer of all who believe.

Encourage me in my anxieties.

Shelter me with your love.

I don't want to meander like a lazy summer river.

I want to rush to your loving embrace

like river rapids in the spring.

THE NEW YEAR

Father Almighty, I commit to you
the new year you have given me.

May those with plenty know love.
May those with little know peace.
Lead all the nations to righteousness.
One soul at a time.

January 21, 2010

THE STORM

One more week until the PET scan.
It's hard to stay in the here and now.

Lord, do you see me?
Do you know I'm here?
Do you know how I feel?

I'm blown here and there
by relentless winds of dread.
So it goes,
from day to night,
from night to day.

Lord, calm the winds.
Bid them be still!

IN GOD'S COCOON

The PET scan reveals cancer in my pelvis.
Here I go again.

Wrap me in a protective cocoon.

There may I grow.

Become strong.

Emerge to glorify you.

ANXIETY

I'm worried about my diagnosis.
My mind is racing
—a mile a minute.

Lord, you see all that is visible,
all that is invisible.
You see all that is outside,
all that is inside.

I dread the oncologist's word
about my treatment.
Why should it matter what he says
if your plan is perfect?

Why am I anxious?
Lord, increase my faith.
Make me strong and steady.

NEEDY

Lots of hustle and bustle around me.
People are worrying about me.

O God, Giver of eternal life and light,

please hear me as I pray.

Without your peace,

without your Holy Spirit,

I feel all alone.

Help me to center my thoughts on you.

Slow down the beat of my heart

to a restful pace.

Sometimes in terror's tempo

I lose touch with you.

SELF-PITY

Self-pity is dangerous.
I'm determined not to let it
pull me down.

Lord Jesus, I'm slipping into self-pity,
I want to honor you.
You love and care for me.
You are my role model.

Lord, I am focusing on my cancer,
drifting into despondency.
I look at others and their problems.
It humbles me in mine.

Lord, take my mind off myself.
Use me to support them.
Let me be their friend.

March 1, 2010

STAND TALL

Another round of chemo now begins.

Your Word is soothing my burning mind.
You have a purpose.
Keep my thoughts focused on you
as I walk through fire once again.

Lord, I live for you.
Help me to stand tall.

COOLING GRACE

Two days after the R-GEMOX chemo.

Gracious God on high,
your truth is my salvation.
Your Word shows me the path to walk.
My body burns, but your grace cools.
Father, give me strength to walk
the path you have chosen.

GOD'S SHINING CURE

Cancer is always in the back
of my mind. It doesn't matter
how long I am in remission.

I cry to you, Lord, as I look around me.

Please hear my voice.

Cradle me and hold me tight.

Father, with you I feel secure.

Peace abounds.

The doctors treat,

but you cure.

Lord, make my murky spirit shine.

Keep me from despair.

March 12, 2010

MORNING COMPASS

I like reading my Bible in the morning.
It steers me in the right direction
before my feet touch the ground.

Lord, you are my compass.

Skillfully,

lovingly,

you point the way,

showing me the direction

I am to go.

STUMBLING

A good-night prayer.

Lord, watch over me tonight
as daylight subsides.
Touch me, so I feel your presence with me.
I need your love. It is my life's potion.
I need your Word. It guides my uneven steps.

March 15, 2010

STRENGTH TO CLIMB

Another day for chemo.
It's a struggle.

Omnipresent Father, you surround all that exists.
You control all outcomes
in the world and beyond.
You are the storehouse of strength.

Once again, as I lower my body
into the gruesome pit of chemotherapy,
I know your love and protection surrounds me.

In the painful pit, I struggle.
You, the ultimate physician, hold me close.
Lord, give me strength to climb out.
Triumphantly.

ROAD MAP

Chemo is finished.
The next appointment
with the oncologist is April 22—a big one.
I have to let it go.
I have to trust God.
He dictates my future.

Some things

I cannot change.

But you can.

Teach me patience.

Give me contentment.

My plans are futile.

You, Lord, have the road map.

GOD'S MERCIES!

PET scan is clear!

Father in heaven,
Thank you for your mercies.
Thank you for your love.
Thank you for your presence,
and your peace!

April 27, 2010

THE PEACEFUL RAIN

I cannot explain God's peace.
It has to be experienced.
It's beyond my understanding.

Lord, thank you for
watering my parched soul.
Strengthening me with your Word.
Your goodness is immeasurable.

Keep me focused on you.
May I stay within the peaceful rain
of your blessings.

May others see you reflected
in all I say and do.

April 30, 2010

A SINKHOLE!

Weak!
My focus is blurred.

My Father in heaven,
In your perfect time,
you will make everything right.

Help me see through the pain.
The side effects of chemo.
The haze that blurs my eyes.
It's hard to focus on what the doctor tells me.
I have no solutions.
I need to concentrate on your Word.

A NARROW PATH

This reprieve from Big C may be short.
I just don't know.

My path is narrow,

filled with peril.

My back carries a heavy weight.

You won't give me more

than I can handle.

May 21, 2010

HOW CAN I SERVE YOU?

Why am I here?
It's for a reason.

Lord, I'm alive because of you.
You are Jehovah-rophe.
You heal.
I love you.
How can I serve you?

PRAYER FOR SUNSHINE

Today is cloudy.

Lord, brighten my day with hope.
My eyes see only darkness.
Give me warmth
as the doldrums
settle on me.
I need to see the sunshine.

June 26, 2010

SERENITY

I think Big C is back.

Give me, Lord, wisdom
to detect your good purposes.
Give me courage
to accept the outcome,
not with rebellion,
not with denial,
but with serenity.

The Prayers

8 7

OTHERS

Doctor appointment today.
As a precaution, he's given me Rituxan
to keep the lymphoma in check.
There are people around me who are less fortunate.
I pray for them.

My strength declines but I refuse

to wallow in despair.

There are many who do.

They have given up.

Their pain is too much.

They are resigned to hopelessness.

May I reach out to them

with words of hope,

with deeds of love.

NEVER ALONE

A PET scan, scheduled
for September 13,
will reveal if Big C is back.
The Lord is with me.
I'm never alone.

As I lie down at night
alone with my pain.
The darkness enfolds me.

Then, your love fills my being.
Startled, I realize I am not alone!

Lord, I want to shout out
your promises
to all who will listen:

"I will never leave you
or forsake you."

"My peace I give to you."

"Do not let your heart be troubled."

WILL IT NEVER END?

The PET scan shows that the cancer is growing.
The lymphoma is persistent.
We are restarting R-GEMOX again.
My doctor is going for a stem cell transplant.

Lord, the battle begins anew.

It never ends.

The pain is relentless.

Weakness.

Fatigue.

In my weariness,

may this be my motto:

Others, Lord—yes, others.

Enable me to help them,

to encourage them,

to pray for them.

CHEMO BRAIN

It's a side effect of chemotherapy.
Some call it Chemo Fog.
Memory problems.
Disorganized.
Can't concentrate.
Frustrating.
Debilitating.

Lord, chemo sends a cloud
over my spirit.

Break through the fog
when I can't think of
the right word.
When I'm confused.
When I can't remember names.
When it takes me forever
to weed the garden.

Lord, break through the haze,
clear my day
to read your Word,
to see your purpose,
to feel your love.

LOOKING UP

Another PET scan is scheduled
for November 19
to see if the chemotherapy
is working.

Lord, you bought me here,

you know the way.

Another storm is brewing.

I look not forward,

but upward.

I am at peace.

LIGHTEN THE DARKNESS

Every Sunday at church
I sense the support of the saints.
They are praying for me.

I am bolstered by and thankful

for the prayers and faith

of these dear ones.

It comforts me.

Hear their prayers.

Lighten my darkness.

Father, hold me tight,

when I am weak in body,

unsure in spirit.

November 11, 2010

THE MYSTERY

Life is not carefree.
A "bowl of cherries"
doesn't apply here.

I may not always
understand your mysteries.
But as they unfold,
the outcome is perfect.

Why is it that
the darker my days,
the brighter your light shines?

94

ETERNAL BRIDGES

WAITING

Another PET scan in two days.
The firing squad will reappear.
Will the bullets miss me?

Father, as I wait
for the oncologists
to decide the next move,
guide their thoughts.

I trust you.
I bow to your wise plan.
I bow to your purposes.

I will accept the verdict.

PET SCAN DAY

The cancer is still there.
Improved, responding to treatment.
However, I need three more
R-GEMOX treatments.

Adrift in the storm,

I am blessed.

Growing in faith,

I have nothing to fear.

I have hope.

I have love.

MY SHELTER

God knows what he's doing.
Healthy habits
(eating, resting,
praying, lots of water)
help me to stay active.
My wonderful wife cares for me
in every possible way.

Lord, I am beat, but not beaten.

My faith is strong, but Satan is persistent.

To you, I trust my life.

With you, I am safe.

With you, I am peaceful.

ACROSS THE BRIDGE

Six cycles of chemotherapy later,
I am physically whipped.
My energy is gone.

Lord, across the dark, cold waters,

you have prepared a bridge for me.

Make my steps sure.

Keep my feet dry.

Smooth the way ahead.

CHRISTMAS EVE

Too weak to stand without getting dizzy,
I've canceled the final chemo treatment.
A cold and fever.
Total exhaustion.
I'm desperate.

Hear my cry, O God,

hear my prayer.

When my heart is overwhelmed,

lead me to the Rock

that is stronger than I.

NEW YEAR'S EVE

The treatments are taking their toll.
I can hardly get out of bed.
I can't stay vertical for very long.

Lord, I'm still crying out to you.

I cry for you all day long.

Life is a constant battle.

I feel like a rotting bag of flesh,

trying to crawl to you.

With the aid of your saints

who hold up my arms,

steady my feet,

I'm slowly moving toward you.

Without you, I can't make it.

ABOVE THE CLOUDS

Starting to feel
a little more normal.
I still have a long way to go.

Lord Jesus, your comforting light
shines brilliantly over the earth for all to see.

Except for me.
I cannot see it.
I am in the valley
of a thick forest
on a cloudy day.

I cannot feel your presence.
I know you are there.
I know your light still shines.
Somewhere above
the trees and clouds.

And I am comforted.

January 17, 2011

HOPE RETURNS

Another PET scan today.

Father, watch over me today.
Shine your healing light on me.
Let it illuminate me,
from the top of my head,
to the tip of my toes.

ALMOST CLEAR

I'm getting closer.
There's a small improvement.
Stem cell transplant is next.
My heart is still weak.
On cardiac meds.

Lord, I am rejoicing.
Your loving mercy,
power, and kindness
overwhelm me.

You are giving me
abundant grace
for all to see.

Your healing light shines
down on me, loosening
the grip of malignancy once again.
Thank you, Lord,
for answering when I pray.
I am forever in your debt.
With every borrowed breath
I will serve you.

IN YOUR NAME

More and more people
are talking to me
about their hard times.
It is my joy to encourage.

Lord, you have brought
many people into my life.
They intersect with me
from every angle
and every walk.

I want to respond to them
lovingly,
patiently,
helpfully.

In your name,
with your wisdom,
and your grace.

Amen.

HIS LOVING ARMS

*The path to the stem cell transplant
has been a long, hard one.
I'll soon be there.
Thanks be to God.*

O Guiding Light from above,

lead me onward.

I will faithfully follow.

Maneuver me right into

your loving arms.

STAYING ON TARGET

The heart medication
is giving me feeling
in my hands and feet.
They have long been numb
from chemotherapy.
April 7 I will know
if I am strong enough
for a stem cell transplant.

Another day has begun.

A painful one.

Side effects from chemo

cling persistently to me.

I don't even want to move.

Yet, I welcome tomorrow.

In reading your Word,

and serving you,

I forget my pain.

I have so much to thank you for.

Cancer is a Life Changer

THERE'S NO WAY AROUND IT. Cancer changes life—for those who endure it and for those who stand by. No easy journey, I can testify to the fact that prayer softens the process. My faith is stronger; my sensitivity to those who are in pain is greater.

I have just completed the stem cell transplant procedure. I cannot feel my feet and so I shuffle. My hands shake, and texting is difficult. Yet my vision is clear.

I now have a new genetic makeup. The statistics say there's a seventy percent likelihood that no cancer remains in my bloodstream. Each day now has a renewed purpose. I'm embarking on a new path marked out by God. I will walk that path, greeting with a smile each person I meet. I want to pray for and encourage those who walk along with me across the bridge into the mysterious ways of God that we do not yet know.

To learn more about how my journey unfolds, look for me on the web at: **www.eternalbridgesprayers.com**.

Please join me. I will continue to write down my thoughts in prayer to God, acknowledging his goodness. I invite you to do so as well. Together, we will journey on.

THE JOURNEY

Lord, I have taken the journey
across dark, cold waters,
in strange surroundings,
through unknown territory
where I have never been before.
You prepared a bridge for me.

You made my steps sure,
kept my feet dry.
You rested your hand on my shoulder,
put my mind at ease.
You smoothed the way ahead.

Father, show me the way
that now lies before me.
Help me to stand firm,
to reach out my hand
to all who need your help.

To care for others
is what I want to do.

Amen.